Table of Contents

Introduction

In the early morning light of October 20th, 2011, a large vehicle convoy hurriedly departed a small residential district in Sirte, Libya in a desperate flight for survival. Within minutes, explosions rocked the path of the vehicles and the convoy splintered. Moments later, as munitions rained from fighter aircraft, a desperate survivor and handful of his loyal men abandoned their vehicles and fled into a nearby farmer's field. Never admitting the possibility of defeat, the frantic fugitive finally sought refuge in a nearby drainage pipe. Opposing ground forces soon converged and pulled a cowering, dazed man from his dusty, rock-strewn hiding place. At the end of a few savage minutes, the forty-two year dictator of Libya, Muammar Gaddafi, was dead.[1]

Gaddafi's death culminated the United States' and North Atlantic Treaty Organization's (NATO) military Operations Odyssey Dawn and Unified Protector, respectively. The operations' impetus was the United Nations Security Counsel Resolutions authorizing force to protect civilians from repressive actions by their own leadership. As coercive goals became codified prior to and during military operations, they contrasted sharply with the resulting events. If the United States and its allies simply intended to effect a behavioral change by Gaddafi, a central question remains: did the United States and its allies successfully apply coercion theory to Libya preceding and during Operations Odyssey Dawn and Unified Protector? If so, why didn't Gaddafi concede instead of ultimately ending up dead outside of a drainage ditch? In other words, did coercion fail? If so, why? This monograph purports that according to stated policy, the United States and its allies did not prefer the tragic unfolding of events but rather compliance. Therefore, even

---

[1]BBC News, "Muammar Gaddafi: How He Died," *BBC news online*, October 31, 2011, http://www.bbc.co.uk/news/world-africa-15390980 (accessed March 21, 2012).

1

though Operations Odyssey Dawn and Unified Protector succeeded in supporting the removal of the Gaddafi regime, ultimately they represent a coercive failure.

The United States holds a storied coercive history with Gaddafi's Libya. In 1981, the Reagan administration demanded Libya stop terrorist activities and its support to terrorists. U.S. naval exercises in the Mediterranean Sea only enflamed the tensions between the two countries.[2] A sharp spike in American deaths to terrorist attacks peaked with the April 1986 Libyan-led bombing of a Berlin discotheque. The U.S. retaliated with airstrikes against Gaddafi's personal compound and other targets in an operation called El Dorado Canyon. Eventually, unilateral sanctions coupled with limited airstrikes created a partial reduction of Libya's overt support to terrorist activities.

The mirage of coercive success, however, quickly vanished in the ashes of the Pan Am Flight 103 bombing in December 1988 at Lockerbie, Scotland. The United States and Britain subsequently demanded the extradition of two bomber suspects. During this period, Libya suffered only limited diplomatic and economic sanctions from the international community.[3] Although Libya did eventually agree to hand over two suspects for trial to the Netherlands in exchange for sanction removal, Gaddafi did not agree to any additional demands of compensation or responsibility for the bombing.

Ongoing talks with Libya continued to focus on its weapons of mass destruction (WMD) program and terrorism until the September 11th attacks dramatically altered the security environment. The Afghanistan invasion and impending invasion of Iraq demonstrated the

---

[2]Phil Haun, "On Death Ground: Why Weak States Resist Great Powers Explaining Coercion Failure in Asymmetric Interstate Conflict" (PhD diss., Massachusetts Institute of Technology, 2010), 367.

[3]Ibid., 368.

credibility of U.S. military action with regards to regime removal. Consequently, not only did Gaddafi finally offer to pay compensation to Pan Am Flight 103 victims' families, he completely conceded his WMD programs and normalized relations with the United States in December 2003.[4] As military actions toppled regimes around him, he seized the opportunity to comply with American demands. In each case, the United States expressed a clear, desired change of behavior. In each case, the United States threatened force or demonstrated an expression of national power to bring about a change of behavior.

If America and Libya's shared coercive experience provides a more distant, historical context for military actions in 2011, the Arab Spring phenomenon provides the immediate backdrop. The rapid eruption of popular protests against autocratic regimes in North Africa and the Middle East surprised the vast majority of academic specialists on the Arab world.[5] After demonstrations associated with the Arab Spring successfully removed Tunisian president Ben-Ali from power, protests soon spread to Egypt, Syria, Bahrain, Syria, Yemen and Libya.[6] In each case, the autocratic governments chose to exercise force to counter the uprising. When Gaddafi ordered his air forces to attack protesters, international outcry against the dictator drew international condemnation. Thus, as Gaddafi reacted forcefully to the effects of Arab Spring sweeping through Libya in early 2011, America and its allies spied the opportunity to exert a behavioral change on the dictator once again.

─────────────────────

[4]Haun, 371.

[5]Greg Gause III, "Why Middle East Studies Missed the Arab Spring: The Myth of Authoritarian Stability," *Foreign Affairs* 90, no. 4 (July/August 2011): 81.

[6]Utz Pape, "Interventions Against a Dictator," *Journal of International Affairs* 65 (Fall/Winter 2011): 221.

However, exact abeyance to coercive demands remained elusive. Seemingly all formal resolutions and mission statements issued from international community were clear enough—the central issue in Libya was the protection of the Libyan people from its own repressive regime. Cessation of repression promised cessation of hostile actions and threats. Yet, Gaddafi, as the target of coercive efforts, did not shift his behavior. Hostilities against the Libyan people did not cease. The central question of this monograph begs, "Why not?" Again, if the United States and its allies attempted to apply coercion theory against Gaddafi preceding and during military operations, why did he end up dead outside of a ditch?

This monograph's hypothesis states that even though Operations Odyssey Dawn and Unified Protector succeeded in supporting the removal of the Gaddafi regime, ultimately they represent a coercive failure as evidenced by a lack of behavioral change by the dictator prior to his death. Because national military guidance clearly sets forth a prominent role for coercion in future policy, it implies a subsequent and continuing need for the United States to understand and properly execute coercive military operations. The 2012 National Military Strategy, *Sustaining U.S. Leadership: Priorities for 21ˢᵗ Century Defense*, describes credible coercion resulting from the "capabilities to deny an aggressor the prospect of achieving his objectives and from the complementary capability to impose unacceptable costs on the aggressor."[7] Coercion relies heavily on the threat of force and the metered use of force less than the full application of all available force. As such, coercion affords a level of efficiency in its use of military forces. Thus, coercion becomes especially critical when U.S. forces are committed to large-scale operations

---

[7] U.S. Department of Defense, *Sustaining U.S. Global Leadership: Priorities for 21ˢᵗ Century Defense* (Washington, DC: Government Printing Office, January 2012), 4. *Sustaining U.S. Leadership* actually uses the term deterrence throughout the document. As used, deterrence falls under a larger theoretical umbrella of coercion, described later.

elsewhere or in budget-constrained environments. Such a situation occurred in 2011 when U.S. and NATO forces participated in operations in Libya even while large-scale operations still existed in Afghanistan and to a limited extent in Iraq. As Operations Odyssey Dawn and Unified Protector potentially demonstrate a recent coercive attempt, they can provide an instructive example of applied coercion theory.

Several potential reasons exist for the disparity between the stated coercive purpose of military actions in Libya and the outcome. One possible explanation could be the misapplication of an otherwise sound coercive theory. In other words, military planners simply chose the wrong approach given the operational environment. Alternatively, a fatal flaw in coercion theory itself could exist. Finally, military operations in Libya potentially might have not represented a coercive attempt at all. This monographs addresses the disparity between the stated coercive purpose of military actions in Libya, the outcome, and the resulting implications.

To this end, this monograph's methodology seeks to understand whether coercion failed and if so, why it failed. It begins by describing historical and conventional coercion theory as well as its evolution in the post-9/11 context. Next, it details Libya's historical and military-political context. It also highlights coalition strategic goals as expressed through institutional statements and resolutions. It then uses historical analysis to discern and describe the coercive attempts by the United States and its coalition partners against the Gaddafi regime. Finally, this monograph correlates the identified coercive methods and the ultimate result. In conclusion, the monograph offers three realizations Libya offers the body of coercive theory and its impact on coercion in practice.

Limitations and Assumptions

Numerous actors interacted during the course the Libyan Civil War of 2011. The United Kingdom, France, the United States and many others played a significant role in the coalition military efforts. Different military structures had separate operational designations for its military actions. For instance, the United States termed its military contribution Operation Odyssey Dawn whereas NATO termed its collective military effort Operation Unified Protector. Because of the significant impact of American and coalition military efforts, discussion using both operational names lends clarity to the historical account. In addition to dissimilar operational designations, coalition warfare necessarily entails differing and occasionally inconsistent national objectives. In order to focus on the effects of coercion towards a common end, this monograph discusses strategic objectives consistent with expressed institutional objectives of the United Nations, NATO, the United States and its coalition partners. At the same time, it recognizes the tensions among nations in regards to specific national objectives.

Furthermore, traditional coercion theory relies on a simplistic, interstate conflict construct. This research, however, acknowledges the existence of a significant and multi-faceted rebel force internal to Libya. Such complexity catalyzed the historical backdrop and drove the narrative throughout the operations. For instance, Libya consists of three broad geographical areas—Tripolitania in the northwest, Fezzan in the southwest, and Cyrenaica in the northeast. Scattered throughout the three regions, ethnically distinct Arabs, Berbers, Tebou, and Touareg people comprise a complex tribal system that consists of over 140 tribal networks.[8] Whereas traditional coercion theory focuses almost exclusively on interstate interactions, the following analysis incorporates influential internal factors.

Finally, the recency of Operations Odyssey Dawn and Unified Protector create classification barriers to research. Operational details such as target sets, official communications and operational intents are necessarily unavailable. This monograph, therefore, derives

---

[8]Christian Science Monitor, "Libya Tribes: Who's Who?" *Christian Science Monitor online,* February 24, 2011, http://www.csmonitor.com/World/Backchannels/2011/0224/Libya-tribes-Who-s-who (accessed September 3, 2012).

operational details from congressional reports, official news sources, and organizational press releases from major institutions such as the U.N., NATO, and AFRICOM.

Coercion Theory

For the purpose of this monograph, the term coercion means efforts to affect a desired behavioral outcome through the use of force, threat of force, or concerted use of both.[9] Thomas Schelling's *Arms and Influence* first brought focus to a coherent coercion theory in 1966. His broad concept of coercion included specific terms such as compellence and deterrence to signify types of desired behavioral outcomes. Compellence seeks to actively alter a target actor's current behavior. Alternatively, deterrence seeks to convince an actor to maintain a status quo. Simply put, compellence urges an actor to stop doing an unfavorable activity; deterrence would have the unfavorable activity never occur. Traditional coercion theory reduces a coercive target to a single rational actor; more recent coercion theory starts to address more complex decision schemas. While in reality, mechanisms to achieve compellence and deterrence often become indistinguishable, the separation of the terms adds clarity to the understanding of military operations and intent in Libya.

Historical Coercion Theory

The practice of coercion predates modern theoretical constructs. As Thucydides described the Peloponnesian War twenty-seven centuries ago, military coercion abounded. Even in the diplomacy of the famed Melian Dialogue, threatened military repercussions informed

---

[9]Thomas C. Schelling, *Arms and Influence* (New Haven, CT: Yale University Press, 1966), 70-71.

decision-making.[10] Coercive thought does not dwell exclusively in classic Western literature. Sun Tzu, the ancient Chinese military philosopher, ascribed the highest praise to the general who could evoke a decision without even fighting.[11] Clearly, statesmen and generals have always considered force and the threat of force a proper mechanism to alter behavior.

Before coercion theory coalesced as a coherent body of thought during the early years of the Cold War, prominent military theorists recognized the basic tenets of forcing one's will onto another. The foremost Western strategic thinker, Carl von Clausewitz, famously acknowledged this when he described war as "an act of force to compel our enemy to do our will."[12] Furthermore, Clausewitz's developed his thoughts on coercion, stating

> If the enemy is to be coerced you must put him in a situation that is even more unpleasant than the sacrifice you call on him to make. The hardships of that situation must not of course be merely transient-or at least not in appearance...Consequently, if you are to force the enemy, by making war on him, to do your bidding, you must make him defenseless or at least put him in a position that makes this danger probable.[13]

Clausewitz subsequently acknowledged that actual fighting need not occur. Mere evaluations of the probability of defeat by the enemy can achieve warfare's aim. Thus, a prominent thinker on war laid the intellectual groundwork for the evolution of coercion theory.

---

[10]Thucydides, *History of the Peloponnesian War* (New York: Penguin, 1954), 402. In the famed Melian Dialogue, the weaker Melians lament to the threatening Athenians: "The strong do what they have the power to do, the weak suffer what they have to accept."

[11]Roger T. Ames, ed. and trans., *Sun Tzu: The Art of Warfare* (New York: Ballantine Books, 1993), 111. Sun Tzu claimed "the highest excellence is to subdue the enemy's army without fighting at all. Therefore, the best military policy is to attack strategies." Targeting an enemy's strategy is discussed later in denial strategy as a subset of coercion theory.

[12]Carl von Clausewitz, *On War*, Edited and Translated by Michael Howard and Peter Paret (Princeton, NJ: Princeton University Press, 1976), 75.

[13]Ibid., 77.

Notably, not all war-generated violence is coercive in nature. Brute force, or unfettered violence, seeks to overwhelm or destroy an enemy completely. A target agreeing to unconditional compliance following a complete defeat is not an example of coercion but rather submission. Coercion must allow for an enemy's decision while his means to resist still reasonably exists.

Modern Coercion Theory

Introduction of nuclear weapons provided a strong impetus for an understanding of coercion, specifically with regards to deterrence. Given the undesirable devastation potentially wrought by nuclear weapons, deterrence emerged as the dominant, but primarily passive means to influence potential threats. Initiative rested with the enemy's first move that would trigger a threatened response from a coercer.[14] Although certainly important, Schelling sensed that deterrence only partially described a more comprehensive coercion theory; he therefore introduced the idea of compellence. Thus, compellence proactively induces an enemy's behavioral change "by an action that threatens to hurt."[15] Therefore, deterrence draws a line and acts if the target crosses it; compellence draws a line behind a target and acts until the target proverbially withdraws behind it.[16]

Once established in the coercive lexicon, the broad terms of deterrence and compellence required further attention. Robert Pape compiles four specific coercive strategies under the

---

[14]Schelling, Arms and Influence, 70.

[15]Ibid., 80.

[16]Walter J. Petersen, "Deterrence and Compellence: A Critical Assessment of Conventional Wisdom," *International Studies Quarterly* 30, no.3 (September 1986): 282.

9

deterrence/compellence umbrella: punishment, risk, denial and decapitation.[17] Punishment, a predominantly Douhetian assertion, attempts to inflict enough pain on civilians to force governmental concessions or risk popular uprising.[18] Byman and Waxman elaborate and expand on Pape's concept of punishment to include multiple "mechanisms" to leverage punishment— namely, powerbase erosion, unrest and weakening.[19] A coercer ought to mete out punishment deliberately and harshly in response to violated demands. Threat of punishment, therefore, depends heavily on the credibility and capability of the coercer. Fear of punishment thus should theoretically affect the decision maker's calculus favorably towards coercive goals.

As an alternative to punishment, a coercer can use risk to affect a targets decision-making. Risk, originally outlined by Schelling, seeks to raise the risk to civilian populations and economic targets compelling concessions to avoid future suffering.[20] Risk resembles punishment very closely with one key difference. Risk avoids Douhet's complete devastation by holding "ultimate ruin in abeyance."[21] Schelling argued that the key to behavior modification is the anticipation of more punishment.[22] Furthermore, risk depends on clear communication between

---

[17]Robert A. Pape, *Bombing to Win: Air Power and Coercion in War* (Ithaca, NY: Cornell University Press, 1996), 57. Pape describes each of these strategies in terms of specific coercive air strategies although they can be useful in the broader military coercion discussion.

[18]Ibid., 59. The concept of directly targeting civilians, especially in terms of airpower, originated with Giulio Douhet's *Command of the Air*. Because he believed that future wars would be total and unrestrained, he advocated civilians as legitimate targets.

[19]Daniel Byman and Matthew Waxman, *The Dynamics of Coercion: American Foreign Policy and the Limits of Military Might* (Cambridge, UK: Cambridge University Press, 2002) , 50.

[20]Schelling, 2.

[21]Pape, 67.

[22]Schelling, 2-3. "To be coercive, violence has to be anticipated...It is the expectation of more violence that gets the wanted behavior, if the power to hurt can get it at all."

the rivals. As Pape notes, "The coercer must signal clearly that the bombing is contingent on the opponent's behavior and will be stopped upon compliance with the coercer's demands."[23] By holding valuable targets at risk to further violence, the strategy of risk should affect the target's decision-making favorably towards coercive goals.

Another approach to alter decision-making is to remove the decision-maker altogether. Decapitation, a concept most closely associated with Colonel John A. Warden III, aims to remove leadership through targeted attacks.[24] In theory, with the stubborn head removed, stubborn resistance will cease, or at least be paralyzed with regards to its national decision-making capabilities. The appeal of precision-guided weapons and promise of minimal resource commitments, decapitation as a strategy has risen in stature, but floundered in results. Pape outlined three reasons for decapitation's unlikely utility in war: difficulty in actually targeting leaders, demonization and exaggeration of leaders' critical role in a state of conflict, and the problematic and unpredictable nature of succession.[25] The result of recent deaths of national or supranational leaders such as Saddam Hussein and Osama Bin Laden demonstrates the tenuous link between defeating a leader and quelling conflict.

The coercion strategies above all seek to impose a cost. Denial, the fourth coercive theory, in contrast, seeks to reduce any benefits of continuing the undesirable behavior. Denial attempts to destroy enough military forces as to deny the enemy's strategy.[26] Thus, denial often blends with the imposition strategies, as targets are struck in a manner consistent with a different

---

[23]Ibid., 67.

[24]Ibid., 79.

[25]Ibid., 81.

[26]Ibid., 69.

strategy. The difference, then, is a matter of degree.[27] If the goal of targeted strikes is to convince, the strategy is denial. If the goal is to physically thwart, the strategy is brute force. By analyzing forty historical case studies, Pape argued that only denial through theater-level attacks has historically provided promise of successful coercion.[28] Byman and Waxman extend the argument to strategic denial: the key is the defeat of an enemy's strategy for victory, not just fielded forces.[29] Denial becomes a moving target as opponents can shift strategies mid-conflict. Only when a target cedes the futility of all available strategies does denial accomplish its final work. Thus, whereas denial may prove the most elusive coercive strategy, it may also prove the most efficacious.

Punishment, risk, decapitation and denial continue to bound discourse concerning coercion. Generally, punishment and risk strategies target that which the population or decision makers hold valuable; decapitation and denial target military forces or the decision makers themselves.[30] Historically, punishment, decapitation, and risk, especially in terms of strategic bombing and air campaigns, have failed to live up to high expectations of their theorists.

Efforts to coerce, regardless of general strategy, must be considered in terms of the enemy's decision making, appreciably an inexact science. In cases of both deterrence and compellence, the target must decide whether or not to comply. Inferably, successful coercion

---

[27]Byman and Waxman, 78.

[28]Pape, 86.

[29]Byman and Waxman, 79.

[30]James R. Cody, "Coercive Airpower in the Global War on Terror: Testing Validity of Courses of Action," (Master's thesis, School of Advanced Military Studies, 2003), 18.

depends on at least two factors: credibility and strength of persuasion.[31] Credibility refers to the coercer's reputation for being willing to carry out threats. Persuasion refers to the coercer's capability to threaten something critically important to the target. In other words, a coercer must demonstrate willingness and capacity to follow through with threats. Clear communication of the threat from the coercer to the target must also accompany credibility and persuasion.

Using credibility, persuasion and communication, ultimately the coercer seeks to convince the target that conceding to demands will be better than refusing them. Alternatively, resistance will hurt more than the price of compliance. As a method to appreciate the relationship between costs, benefits and their probabilities, Pape advocated an overly simple decision calculus equation. Whereas, the formula does not address the complexities of the real world, it provides an insight to basic cost-benefit relationships.

$$R = B*p(B) - C*p(C)$$

where:
- R = value of resistance
- B = benefits of resistance
- $p(B)$ = probability of attaining benefits of continued resistance
- C = potential costs of resistance
- $p(C)$ = probability of suffering costs.[32]

If the value of resistance drops to less than zero, concessions theoretically occur. The coercer must decipher which variables become reasonably effectible. However, the decision remains with the target that determines if the cost (in light of the probability of the reckoning) is less than the fruits of resistance (in light of the probability of the resistance succeeding). The use of an equation does not imply quantitative values in situations that are highly uncertain and inherently qualitative. Clearly a danger exists in trying to quantify the unquantifiable. Rather, decision

---

[31]Patrick Bratton, "When is Coercion Successful, and Why Can't We Agree On It?" *Naval War College Review* 58, no. 3 (Summer 2005): 101.

[32]Pape, 16.

calculus intends to demonstrate a simple relationship between cost and benefit in the decision-maker's mind.

Decision calculus implies an opportunity by the target to positively respond to the messages and signals of the coercer. Communication, previously described as requiring clarity and credibility, additionally requires an authentic desire to accommodate a coerced decision. A capability to accommodate a coerced response provides the foundation for a successful coercion. A desire to accommodate a coerced response is required to even qualify a military operation as a coercive attempt.

The end of the Cold War fundamentally shifted thinking with regard to coercion theory. In a primarily hegemonic system, the United States focused on coercion in the context of smaller, regional, and certainly conventional conflicts. Contemporary examples of coercion include military actions in Kosovo, Bosnia, and Iraq including Operations Desert Storm, Northern Watch and Southern Watch. If deterrence, especially nuclear deterrence, served as the chief problem of the Cold War, conventional compellence has served as the chief problem of the post-Cold War era.[33]

Following the attacks on the World Trade Center in September 2001, coercion theory adjusted again. Writers questioned the relevance of the dominant Cold War interpretations of deterrence and compellence in light of non-state actors and terrorist organizations.[34] Even in interstate contexts, questions emerged with regards to overly simplistic assumptions of a unitary, rational decision maker. One approach, called synthetic cognitive modeling, represented efforts to

---

[33]Pape, 329.

[34]Paul K. Davis, *Simple Models to Explore Deterrence and More General Influence in the War with al-Qaeda* (Arlington, VA: RAND Corporation, 2010): 1. Davis observes that al-Qaeda leaders display a different rationality, if not an irrational zeal, in decision-making. For this and other reasons, he concludes that military strategists could not use traditional coercion theory when dealing with transnational terrorists.

avoid simplistic decision attribution to a potential enemy.[35] This thinking advocated that in real-world crises, complex mixtures of behaviors occur vice simple, calculable responses.

A theory of crony attack also emerged to offer an improved understanding of a complex decision-making environment. Crony attack advocates inflicting cost (or threatening to do so) on those who have the most influence on the decision maker. It seeks leverage on an otherwise immovable actor. As an example of crony attack, an argument has been made that NATO campaign properly and successfully exerted influence on Milosevic's wife and other key power brokers in the ruling coalition during Operation Allied Force in 1999.[36] While not necessarily comprehensive, crony attack starts to address the complexity of decision-making.

In addition to crony attack theory, other theories attempt to explain the variance of decision-making characteristics in different regime types. Selectorate theory, while holding to the obvious assertion that democratic governments and autocratic regimes will respond differently to conflict decisions, introduces the concept of high loyalty within the "selectorate", or those eligible to participate in politics.[37] The complex composition of governments and decision influence drastically alters the notion of decision-making. Such recent strides expand coercion theory beyond a rational, unitary decision maker. Indeed, an over-simplistic, fallacious view of a single, rational actor may actually prove counter-productive to coercive efforts in a complex, evolving world stage.

---

[35]Ibid., 5. Davis concluded that it is "dangerous to assess the enemy (or ourselves) as being single-minded, consistent, coherent, and logical." He offered systems explanations for increasing understanding of efforts, motivations and causation.

[36]Julian Tolbert, "Crony Attack: Strategic Attack's Silver Bullet?" (thesis, School of Advanced Air and Space Studies, 2003), 15.

[37]Richard Andres, "When to Target Enemy Heads of State" (paper presented at the Air Command and Staff College conference on Airpower, Maxwell AFB, AL, Spring 2004).

In spite of the breadth of theoretical discourse, coercive thought generally agrees on several tenets. First, because compellence has a positive aim while deterrence has a negative aim, compellence tends to be more difficult than deterrence.[38] In other words, action possesses an inertial component. Thus, an undesirable behavior is easier to modify prior to activity than after it. Additionally, for coercion to work, a coercer must skillfully impose certain conditions. First, the target should believe that resistance is futile; strategy denial relates closely to this tenet.[39] Second, the target should believe that denying compliance offers no further benefits.[40] Furthermore, immediate compliance should appeal more than delayed compliance.[41] In other words, the pain will continue to increase. Additionally, compliance must include an authentic "way out" offer within the ability of the target to respond. Finally, the communicated terms of compliance must seem palatable to decision makers. The last condition points out a potentially fatal flaw in coercion theory: conceding to a coercer's demands may literally represent a death sentence for many a decision maker.[42] This obstacle may provide sufficient cause to resist regardless of other threatened costs. All of these issues factor into a leader's decision-making calculus.

---

[38]Pape, *Bombing to Win*, 6. Lawrence Freedman, *Deterrence* (Cambridge, UK: Polity Press, 2006): 110. Karl Mueller, "The Essence of Coercive Air Power: A Primer for Military Strategists," *Air Power Journal* 2, no. 1 (Spring 2007): 160. Mueller also argues that compellence and deterrence can be misconstrued through semantics and should be considered two ends of a continuum vice two distinct categories.

[39]Mueller, 173.

[40]Ibid., 174.

[41]Ibid.

[42]Ibid.

Lawrence Freedman adds a final note on post-9/11 coercive thought. He asserts that in a modern, complex international order, force and the threat of force play a normative role in a state actor's behavior. In other words, "to the extent that the possible use of force is part of these processes of norm-setting," policies of deterrence and compellence can be drawn upon.[43] He adds that the concept of norm setting does not precisely follow classic deterrence theory, but rather draws on the old debates. Norms-based thought with regards to coercion centers on the long duration behavioral modification of an actor, not an immediate response to a carrot or a stick as Pape's decision calculus formula might suggest. In such a manner potential actors mend unacceptable behavior not from a "sharp adjustment in the course of an immediate crisis, but through the internalization of the norms to the point where they no longer need external reinforcement."[44]

Attempts to compel an enemy to another's will are as old Pericles and as recent as Gaddafi. Early coercion theories, like those advocated by Pape and Schelling, provide a simple understanding of compellence, deterrence, denial, punishment, decapitation and risk. Recent elaborations and adaptations of coercion theory allow for more complex models that expand beyond unitary, rational decision-making and beyond an immediate crisis. In all cases, coercion theory takes into account any military force or threat of force, short of brute force-induced compliance, which seeks to change a behavior while means to resist still exist. If the United States and its allies intended to elicit a behavioral change and not simply forced compliance in 2011, then coercion theory can increase the understanding of an interested student as to the utility of their actions in light of the Libyan responses.

---

[43]Freedman, 130.

[44]Ibid.

Historical Analysis

To view American and NATO military actions against Libya through the lens of coercion theory, one must understand the unfolding events preceding and during Operations Odyssey Dawn and Unified Protector. The Arab Spring in Libya, Gaddafi's initial actions, the coalition's response and operational approach, and Gaddafi's responses to coalition actions and demands all help to inform an understanding of the applicability of coercion in the Libyan context.

Arab Spring in Libya

Emboldened by political uprisings in Tunisia and Egypt, popular protests against Gaddafi's government began in earnest mid-February 2011. Groups opposed to Gaddafi's regime called for "a day of rage" with protests scheduled for 17 February to commemorate protests from five years prior.[45] The popular unrest, however, erupted in the days preceding the planned protests. On 15 February a large number of protesters gathered in Benghazi, the largest city in eastern Libya. Libyan police forces responded with tear gas, water cannons and rubber bullets.[46] In spite of the police forces' seemingly restrained responses and calls for redress in proper channels of communication, protests quickly spread to other towns in eastern Libya. By the time of the planned "day of rage" protests on February 17th, general outrage subsumed the eastern towns of Libya.

Having spread from Benghazi to Beyida, Zentan, Darnah, and Rijban, protests wrought new and deadly responses from the Libyan government. During the "day of rage" protests,

---

[45]Christopher Blanchard, *Libya: Unrest and U.S. Policy* (Washington DC: Congressional Research Service, March 29, 2011), 1.

[46]Al Arabiya News, "Clash Breaks Out as Libya Braces for Day of Anger," *Al Arabiya online*, February 16, 2011, http://www.alarabiya.net/articles/2011/02/16/137834.html (accessed May 27, 2012).

security forces and snipers used live ammunition against protesters.[47] In the following days, military helicopters reportedly attacked gatherings of protesters with live ammunition.[48] Additional evidence mounted that Gaddafi had ordered his military to suppress the uprising by attacking civilian gatherings. Libyan fighter jets also attacked protesters. When two Libyan fighter pilots defected in their aircraft following orders to directly attack civilians, the Gaddafi regime became publicly and undeniably complicit in its use of the military to use deadly force against its own people.[49]

By late February, protests had spread from the eastern cities to the steps of the capitol in Tripoli. Strong repressive measures in the capitol meant that Tripoli would remain in government control for the time being. Yet Gaddafi had lost control of a significant portion of Libya by the end of March including the major cities of Benghazi, Tobruk, Misrata, and the port of Brega.[50] Additionally, the resignations of key government and military figures threatened to weaken Gaddafi's position of power.[51] Resignations included the country's interior minister, a senior aide to Gaddafi's son Saif al-Islam Gaddafi, multiple general officers and the country's justice

---

[47]USA Today, "Anti-government Protesters Killed in Libyan Clash," *USA Today online*, February 17, 2011, http://www.usatoday.com/news/world/2011-02-17-libya-protests_N htm (accessed on May 27, 2012).

[48]Sudarson Raghaven and Leila Fadel, "Military Helicopters Reportedly Fire on Protesters in Libya," *Washington Post online*, February 21, 2011, http://www.washingtonpost.com/wp-dyn/content/article/2011/02/20/AR2011022004185.html (accessed on May 27, 2012).

[49]Ibid.

[50]Al Jazeera, "Gaddafi Defiant as State Teeters," *Al Jazeera online*, February 23, 2011, http://www.aljazeera.com/news/africa/2011/02/20112235434767487 html, (accessed on May 28, 2012).

[51]Ibid.

minister; additionally, a Libyan diplomat to the United Nations called on the Libyan army to help remove Gaddafi from power.[52] Libya teetered on the brink of collapse or civil war.

The international community countered quickly to the Libyan protests and their government's violent reactions. Early diplomatic responses included the U.S. State Department withdrawing all non-essential diplomats and embassy family members from Libya.[53] Furthermore, United Nations Secretary General Ban Ki-moon communicated directly with Gaddafi and emphasized that the violence must stop immediately.[54] National and international condemnation and calls for cessation of hostilities forthwith materialized.

Given the increasing violence, instability, and international pressure, the United Nations Security Council adopted its first resolution regarding Libya on February 26, 2011—Resolution 1970. In essence, UNSCR 1970 imposed an arms embargo restricting arms import and export as well as the transit of mercenaries into Libya.[55] The resolution also gave the International Criminal Court jurisdiction over crimes committed in Libya, subjected Gaddafi and other regime figures to travel bans and financial forfeiture, and called for humanitarian assistance from the international community.[56] Notably, UNSCR 1970 threatened increased sanctions on any individual who threatened or caused increased human rights abuses, specifically "attacks and aerial bombardments on civilian populations."[57] Most importantly, this resolution served as an initial

---

[52]Ibid.

[53]Sudarson Raghaven, "Military Helicopters," *Washington Post online.*

[54]Ibid.

[55]United States Mission to the United Nations, *Fact Sheet: UN Security Council Resolution 1970, Libya Sanctions*, http://usun.state.gov/briefing/statements/2011/157194.htm, (accessed on 28 May, 2012).

[56]Ibid.

[57]Ibid.

platform from which the Security Council and the international community would continue to refine its demands and responses to Gaddafi's actions in Libya.

A day after the adoption of the Security Council Resolution 1970, opposition to Gaddafi's government coalesced into a viable organization. Founded on 27 February, the National Transitional Council (NTC) became the focal organization to coordinate resistance among rebel held towns.[58] Initially, the council intended to serve as an umbrella organization for disparate factions, not as an interim government.[59] It's vision for itself quickly grew from a coordinating body into the only true legitimate governing body for the Libyan people.[60] Nonetheless, Gaddafi now faced a full-blown rebellion with a unified, political body.

In early March, Gaddafi responded strongly to the threat to his power. He vowed to "die as a martyr" on Libyan soil and rallied loyal supporters to his cause.[61] A renewed offensive saw government forces successfully drive towards eastern Libyan cities held by rebel forces. In mid-March, as Gaddafi's forces approached Benghazi, the entire opposition movement faced defeat.

Coalition Narrative/Strategic Goals

As the resistance against the Libyan government stammered, the United States sought to increase diplomatic pressure to change Gaddafi's behavior. In late February and early March,

---

[58]Al Jazeera, "Libyan Opposition Launches Council", *Al Jazeera online*, February 27, 2011, http://www.aljazeera.com/news/africa/2011/02/2011227175955221853 html# (accessed on May 28, 2012).

[59]Ibid.

[60]The Interim National Council, "A Vision of a Democratic Libya," *Al Jazeera online*, March 29, 2011, http://www.aljazeera.com/mritems/Documents/2011/3/29/201132911392394381lThe%20Interim %20Transitional%20National%20Council%20Statement.pdf (accessed on May 30, 2012).

[61]"Libyan Opposition Launches Council," *Al Jazeera online*.

President Obama officially shifted the US policy with Libya away from *rapprochement.*[62]

Rapprochement is the easing of tensions or reestablishment of a friendly relationship.

Rapprochement had been implemented in 2003 following Libya's agreement to cease weapons of

mass production pursuance. In coercive terms, rapprochement offered benefits of cooperation to a

decision-maker. In light of Gaddafi's violence against his citizens, instead of continued

rapprochement, the United States, via executive order, placed financial freezes on Libyan assets

and interactions in response to the governmental crackdown on its civilians.[63] Yet, other than the

reversal of rapprochement, in late February and early March President Obama did not specify the

steps the United States intended to take to help create a coercive outcome. The political aims of

the United States remained unclear.

In early March, the Arab community began to consolidate its approach to the Libyan

crisis. On March 12, the Arab League asked the United Nations to create a no-fly zone over Libya

to protect civilians. In a statement declaring that Gaddafi government had "lost its sovereignty,"

the Arab League specifically called for the U.N. to "shoulder its responsibility" and "impose a

no-fly zone over Libya to protect civilians from air attack."[64] The call for a no-fly zone centered

on the vulnerability of civilians to violent air attacks.

The international community also sought increased diplomatic or military responses to

change Gaddafi's behavior. Hastened by the faltering resistance movement in early March, the

---

[62]Dana Moss and Ronald Bruce, "Reforming the Rogue: Lessons from the US-Libyan Rapprochement", *The Cutting Edge*, January 4, 2010 http://www.thecuttingedgenews.com/index.php?article=11878&pageid=13&pagename=Analysis (accessed on June 1, 2012).

[63]Blanchard, 1.

[64]United States Africa Command, "Overview of 1st Day of U.S. Operations to Enforce U.N. Resolution 1973 Over Libya", *USAFRICOM Public Affairs Release*, 20 March 2011, http://www.africom. mil/getarticle.asp?art=6237& (accessed on 28 May, 2011).

United Nations passed UNSCR 1973 on March 17, 2011. The critical authorizations of UNSCR 1973 were the authorization of force and the implementation of a no-fly zone. The new resolution allowed states to take "all necessary measures" to protect civilians and civilian populations under threat of attack.[65] Equally important, it also implemented a no-fly zone over Libya presumably to protect civilian populations from attacks from military aircraft. Other authorizations in the new resolution reinforced or expanded previously adopted articles such as arms embargos, frozen assets, and travel restrictions. Principally, UNSCR 1973 provided the legal foundation and international legitimacy for military operations against the government of Libya.

On the heels of UNSCR 1973, President Obama enumerated non-negotiable demands to Gaddafi to end the violence. The President demanded that "a cease-fire must be implemented immediately, and all attacks against civilians must stop."[66] He further specified that "Qaddafi must stop his troops from advancing on Benghazi, pull them back from Ajdabiya, Misrata, and Zawiya, and establish water, electricity and gas supplies to all areas. Humanitarian assistance must be allowed to reach the people of Libya."[67]

During this same time, the president began to tamp down military and end state expectations with his rhetoric concerning how much force the United States was willing to commit and for which purpose. Foundational to the anticipated approach in Libya, President Obama clearly eliminated the possibility of American ground troops into Libya.[68] Further, he consistently reiterated the aim of U.S. policy as focused on the protection of innocent civilians.

---

[65]United States Mission to the United Nations, *Fact Sheet: New UN Security Council Resolution on Libya*, http://usun.state.gov/briefing/statements/2011/158614 htm, (accessed on 28 May, 2012).

[66]Blanchard, 8.

[67]Ibid.

[68]Ibid.

Specifically, he promised to limit the use of force so as to not exceed the well-defined goal of protecting Libyan civilians.

The American president's focus and limitations nested well with the concept of NATO's No Fly Zone. The U.N. sanctioned the NATO No Fly Zone with a primary purpose to close Libyan airspace to all flights except those delivering humanitarian aid thus preventing attacks from the air against civilian populations.[69] NATO saw its role in Operation UNIFIED PROTECTOR as the military operator part of a "broader international effort to protect the Libyan people from their own government's violence."[70] Primarily a passive mission to deny use of airspace, NATO stated that force was to be used only as a last resort. Nonetheless, NATO acknowledged the right to self-defense against air and ground attacks. Furthermore, NATO vaguely referred to putting pressure on those forces that attack civilians. Thus, force and the threat of force balanced precariously between last resort, self-defense, and a notion of pressuring ground troops.

As military operations continued, NATO continued to refine its message. Force as the last resort seemed to fade as a constraining factor for operations. In response to allegations that NATO air forces intervened on the side of rebellion forces, NATO continued to link its actions to UNSCR 1973's mandate to protect civilians.[71] Yet the purpose of the no-fly zone seemed to have grown from protecting the civilian population from attack to actively destroying threats to

---

[69]NATO, Fact Sheet: Operation UNIFIED PROTECTOR Protection of Civilians and Civilian-Populated Areas & Enforcement of the No-Fly Zone, http://www nato.int/cps/en/natolive/71679 htm., (accessed on 28 May 2011).

[70]Ibid.

[71]BBC News, "NATO Answers Libya Questions," *BBC news online*, August 20, 2011, http://www.bbc.co.uk/ news/world-africa-14603245 (accessed on March 23, 2012). "All the targets are clearly identified as having a direct link with attacks on civilians."

civilians. With respect to the extent that air strikes against government forces aided rebel advances, NATO insisted that any benefit the rebels received was an unintended consequence of strikes against forces threatening civilians.[72] Thus, NATO deflected the notion that it served as the rebel forces' personal air force.[73] Furthermore, NATO insisted that it "had no direct contact with the military forces of the opposition."[74] NATO therefore seemed to maintain its stance as a neutral protector of Libyan civilians.

Subordinate commands quickly nested under U.S. and coalition guidance. U.S. Africa Command (AFRICOM) commanded the American military response in support of the international enforcement of UNSCR 1973. AFRICOM stated its goals as the protection of innocent civilians, prevention of attacks against civilian communities, and the deterrence of mass atrocities.[75] AFRICOM's Commander, General Carter Ham, reiterated his clear military objectives: implementation of a cease-fire including attacks against civilians, withdrawal of troops from the immediate vicinity of Benghazi and other eastern Libyan cities, and the free flow of humanitarian supplies.[76] In support of the broad objectives, AFRICOM's immediate aims became the prevention of further attacks on civilians and opposition groups and the degradation

---

[72]Ibid.

[73]Ibid. NATO claimed that although it tracked the fighting between the forces, it was not involved in the ground battle. Thus NATO, preferring to focus on its actions protecting civilians, attempted to distance its actions from the air with the land battle's outcome.

[74]Ibid.

[75]United States Africa Command, "AFRICOM Commander on Commencement of Military Strikes in Libya," *USAFRICOM Public Affairs Release*, March 19, 2011, http://www.africom.mil/ getArticle.asp?art=6222&lang=0 (accessed on May28, 2011).

[76]Ibid.

of Gaddafi's ability to resist the internationally mandated no-fly zone.[77] The U.S. military operation in support of the international effort was called Operation ODYSSEY DAWN.

Coalition Operational Response

Military actions should support stated political and strategic objectives. Combined, the UNSCR 1973, NATO's No-Fly Zone and USAFRICOM's military objectives provided the organizing principles for military operations in Libya: the implementation of a cease-fire including attacks against civilians, withdrawal of troops from the immediate vicinity of Benghazi and other eastern Libyan cities, and the free flow of humanitarian supplies. Thus, military actions should have systematically supported these lines of effort. By enumerating military actions in Libya, perhaps patterns of coercive intents can emerge.

Coalition military operations began within two days of the passage of UNSCR 1973. Late March 19th, coalition forces launched more than 120 Tomahawk cruise missiles from U.S. and British vessels.[78] The Pentagon quickly asserted that the Tomahawks targeted more than twenty integrated air defense facilities long the coast. In addition to the cruise missiles, coalition aircraft also penetrated Libyan airspace for the first time on the evening of 19 March including fifteen U.S. strike and electronic warfare aircraft.[79] Targets of the initial wave of attacks also included military airfields such as the one at Misrata, in an effort to emasculate any threat to air operations from the meager Libyan air force.[80]

---

[77]Ibid.

[78]USAFRICOM, "Overview of 1st Day."

[79]Ibid.

[80]BBC News, "Libya: US, France and UK attack Gaddafi Forces," *BBC news online*, 20 Mar 2011, http://www.bbc.co.uk/news/world-africa-12796972 (accessed on September 3, 2012).

The initial airstrikes follow the logic of recent military patterns of quickly achieving air superiority. The U.S. Department of Defense defines air superiority as the "degree of dominance in the air battle by one force that permits the conduct of its operations at a given time and place without prohibitive interference from air and missile threats."[81] Air superiority in almost any contested environment takes priority. Enforcement of a no-fly zone necessarily must operate free from both ground and air threats. Thus, in the context of a no-fly zone, air superiority becomes simultaneously a prerequisite and an objective.

While cruise missiles targeted integrated air defense sites to allow freedom of movement to coalition aircraft, other initial targeting included fielded military forces. French fighter aircraft targeted tanks and other armored vehicles associated with Libyan military forces that immediately threatened the embattled rebels near Benghazi.[82] Whereas governmental forces certainly threatened civilians inside of Benghazi, the military threat to a viable rebel military cannot be overstated. At the initiation of military intervention Libyan governmental forces had eliminated substantial rebel gains in much across much of Libya. Only Benghazi stood as a significant rebel hold out on 19 March 2011. Therefore, the targeting of tanks and armored vehicles seemingly sought to culminate the Libyan government's offensive into Benghazi to allow the rebels time and space for future military operations in addition to protecting civilians from governmental attack.

The initial strikes focused on air defense sites to directly enable the no fly-zone and support UNSCR 1973. The Arab League had called for the coalition to impose a no-fly zone over

---

[81]United States Department of Defense, Joint Publication 1-02, *Dictionary of Military and Associated Terms* (July 15, 2012, repr., Washington DC: Government Printing Office, 8 November 2010) (Amended through, 13.

[82] "Libya: US, France and UK attack Gaddafi Forces," *BBC news online.*

the movement of Libyan military airplanes to create safe zones in the places vulnerable to airstrikes. In the first waves of air strikes, the coalition was well on its way to eliminating the ability of Gaddafi to strike his people through the medium of the air. Through the initial strikes against the integrated air defenses and airfields, the coalition sought to deny Gaddafi any military capability of stamping out the rebellion with air assets while providing freedom of movement for coalition aircraft. Interestingly, by striking military forces surrounding Benghazi, the initial strikes simultaneously protected the civilians inside Benghazi from military attack while reducing Gaddafi's ability to snuff out the rebel's last strong hold. Additionally, following the initial strikes, U.S. Vice Admiral William Gortney, director of the Joint Staff, stressed that strikes were not specifically targeting Gaddafi himself but the structure of the air defense systems.[83] Military operations, at least initially, focused on the enabling of the no fly zone.

Gaddafi's Responses

In the weeks leading up to the initial NATO attacks, Gaddafi bolstered his defiant rhetoric apparently to deter military intervention. He claimed that the government would be victorious; that he would never leave the country; and that he would arm a million citizens to defend Libya.[84] However, as military intervention loomed, his rhetoric shifted towards acquiescence.

---

[83]U.S. Department of Defense, "DOD News Briefing with Vice Adm. Gortney from the Pentagon on Libya Operation Odyssey Dawn," Office of the Secretary of Defense (Public Affairs), 19 March 2011, http://www.defense.gov/transcripts/transcript.aspx?transcriptid=4786 (accessed on 4 September 2012).

[84]Daily Mail, "RAF strikes against Gaddafi's forces branded 'a success' as bombed out tanks and cars litter the roads near Benghazi," *DailyMail online*, March 20, 2011, http://www.dailymail.co.uk/news/article-1368028/Libya-RAF-strikes-Gaddafis-forces-branded-successnearBenghazi html?openGraphAuthor=%2Fhome%2Fsearch.html%3Fs%3D%26authornamef%3DDaily%2BMail%2BReporters (accessed on September 3, 2012).

In immediate response to the passage of UNSCR 1973 on 17 March, Libyan Foreign Minister Musa Kusa signaled that Libya was obligated to abide by the United Nations' resolution and announced an immediate ceasefire by Libyan forces.[85] However, if guns surrounding the embattled city of Benghazi fell silent, they did not stay silent for long. In spite of Kusa's claim to abide by the ceasefire, Libyan governmental ground forces immediately reengaged with rebel ground forces in Benghazi. Claims on both sides accused the other of breaking the ceasefire and forcing a response of self-defense. It is impossible to determine if the ceasefire failed because of a lack of adequate command and control to enforce it at the lowest levels, or it was intentionally broke by either side. The Libyan government may have sought to capitalize surprise in the midst of a ceasefire. The rebels might have easily spoiled the respite to spoil opportunities for Gaddafi to extricate himself from the conditions of the ceasefire. Either way, persistent conflict preceded and made unavoidable the U.S. and coalition military operations on 19 March.

As NATO struck military forces around Benghazi and air defense sites, across Libya Gaddafi immediately decried the military intervention. He claimed that the government would be victorious over these modern crusades.[86] Yet, in spite of his rhetorical bravado in the face of NATO's aerial onslaught, Gaddafi attempted to enact a second ceasefire. He announced early on March 20th that a ceasefire would go into place starting that evening.[87] Again, the attempted ceasefire failed to take hold as fighting continued between the rebels and the Libyan armed forces. All the while Libyan government pleaded for international observers to witness their observation of the ceasefire.

_____

[85]BBC News, "Libya: US, France and UK attack Gaddafi Forces," *BBC news online*, March 20, 2011, http://www.bbc.co.uk/news/world-africa-12796972 (accessed on September 3, 2012).

[86]Daily Mail, "RAF strikes against Gaddafi's forces."

[87]Ibid.

Following an increase of attacks on Libyan tanks and armored forces in early April, calls

for ceasefires again came to a head. The African Union (AU) led negotiations for an immediate

ceasefire that addressed violence and humanitarian aid, the primary catalysts for international

military intervention. [88] However, the NTC rejected the proposal out of hand because the

initiative did not include the departure of Gaddafi and his sons. "Any future proposal that does

not include this, we cannot accept," he said.[89] The White House response agreed with the NTC—

there could be no political agreement without the removal of Gaddafi.[90] The tension between

military operations based on institutional claims of civilian protection and political conditions of

Gaddafi's removal started to become evident at this time. This signified an important transition in

the conception of objectives and future conditions.

Nonetheless, NATO continued to advance the concept of limited and distinct aims. In

April, the commander of the NATO operation, Canadian Lt. Gen. Charles Bouchard, insisted that

the goal of the airstrikes was to "protect civilians, not to work hand-in-hand with the rebels."[91] To

back up his claim, he asserted that NATO enforced the no fly zone on both sides noting that a

NATO aircraft had intercepted a rebel fighter aircraft; it was, incidentally, the only aircraft to be

---

[88]Hadeel Al- Shalchi and Sebastian Abbot, "Libya Cease-Fire: South Africa Says Gaddafi Has Accepted African Union 'Road Map'," *Huffington Post online*, http://www.huffingtonpost.com/2011 /04/10/libya-cease-fire-road-map_n_847226.html, 20 April 2011 (accessed on September 5, 2012).

[89]Leila Fadel, "Libyan rebels reject African Union cease-fire proposal," *Washington Post online*, April 10, 2011, http://www.washingtonpost.com/world/gaddafi-accepts-road-map-for-peace-proposed-by-african-leaders/2011/04/10/AFbrtuJD_story.html (accessed on September 5, 2012).

[90]Ibid. "The Obama administration echoed the rebels' insistence on Gaddafi's departure as a precondition for any political settlement. 'It's a non-negotiable demand,' State Department spokesman Mark Toner told reporters at a Monday news briefing. 'We believe he needs to depart power.'"

[91]Rueters, "NATO forces destroy 25 Libyan tanks," *DefenceWeb online*, April 11, 2011, http://www.defenceweb.co.za/index.php?option=com_content&view=article&id=14711:nato-forces-destroy-25-libyan-tanks&catid=50:Land&Itemid=105 (accessed on September 5, 2012).

intercepted during the military operation.[92]At least officially, NATO still claimed it based its

military operations on the protection of civilians.

In May, Gaddafi seemed to relent and offered a ceasefire with the rebels that would have

enabled humanitarian relief and initiated negotiations with rebels—but entailed no regime

change. NATO and the NTC rejected the offer without consideration…it became clear regime

change had to go. In June, NATO introduced attack helicopters signifying an operational shift

from fighter based air support.[93] Attack helicopters seemingly provided more direct supporting

role for rebel ground forces especially in urban environments where fighter aircraft are less adept.

About this time the air campaign exhibited a significant shift. By late May, NATO had

accumulated over 2,500 airstrikes and increasingly the focus became targets in Tripoli.[94] With

obvious military targets previously struck, the targeted strikes migrated into the Gaddafi's capitol

and neighborhoods, the heart of the old regime. Significantly, NATO aircraft struck directly at

Gaddafi's residential compound reported killing one of his sons and three grandchildren.[95]

Meanwhile, Lieutenant-General Charles Bouchard, commander of Operation Unified Protector,

maintained, "All NATO's targets are military in nature and have been clearly linked to the...

---

[92]Rueters, "NATO forces destroy 25 Libyan tanks."

[93]Varun Vira and Anthony H. Cordesman, "The Libyan Uprising," *Center for Strategic and International Studies*, June 2011, http://csis.org/publication/libyan-uprising-uncertain-trajectory (accessed on September 6, 2012).

[94]John F. Burns, "NATO Bombs Tripoli in Heaviest Strike Yet," *New York Times online*, May 23, 2011, http://www.nytimes.com/2011/05/24/world/africa/24libya.html (accessed on August 12, 2012).

[95]Al Jazeera, "Nato strike 'kills Gaddafi's youngest son'," *Al Jazeera online*, May 1, 2011, http://www.aljazeera.com/news/africa/2011/04/2011430224755721620 html (accessed on September 6, 2012).

regime's systematic attacks on the Libyan population and populated areas. We do not target individuals."[96] Certainly, leadership compounds also serve as command and control nodes.

In response to the Tripoli strikes, Gaddafi remained defiant. "We will not surrender, we will not give up. We have one option—our country. We will remain in it 'til the end. Dead, alive, victorious, it doesn't matter."[97] In May, Gaddafi had offered a ceasefire with the rebels that would have enabled humanitarian relief and initiated negotiations with rebels—but entailed no regime change. NATO and the NTC rejected the offer without consideration. Very little discussion of ceasefires or alternative solutions emerged after May. It had become clear regime change and Gaddafi's removal was the only palatable solution. By15 July, over thirty countries recognized NTC as the legitimate government of Libya.[98] Although tactical success for NATO nor the NTC was not a foregone conclusion, the basis of political acceptability certainly was. Still, NATO Secretary General Anders Fogh Rasmussen said recently that his forces have made "significant progress" in its U.N. Security Council mandate to protect Libyan civilians.[99]

Rebel held territory expanded from the east towards the west, eventually surrounding mere pockets of government supporting troops. By late October, NATO aircraft had flown over 26,500 sorties, including 9,700 strike sorties.[100] Strike sorties are those that actually engaged or

---

[96]Ibid.

[97]CNN Wirestaff. "Gadhafi: We Will Not Surrender, We Will Not Give Up," *CNN online*, June 7, 2011, http://articles.cnn.com/2011-06-07/world/libya.war_1_airstrikes-libyan-officialsnato?_s=PM: WORLD (accessed on August 12, 2012).

[98]Ian Black, "Libyan rebels win international recognition as country's leaders," *Guardian online*, July 15, 2011, http://www.guardian.co.uk/world/2011/jul/15/libyan-rebels-international-recognition-leaders (accessed on September 6, 2012).

[99]Ibid.

[100]NATO, Fact Sheet: Operation UNIFIED PROTECTOR.

were available to engage enemy targets. Aircraft struck over 5,900 military targets including "over 400 artillery or rocket launchers and over 600 tanks or armored vehicles."[101] Gaddafi's loyal military forces were unable to defend against the advancing rebel forces primarily because of the constant bombardment from coalition aircraft. By late September, only the towns of Sirte, Bani Walid and Al Fuqaha remained under the control of forces loyal to Gaddafi. On 20 October 2011, a NATO aircraft targeted a vehicle convoy near Sirte transporting a fleeing Gaddafi. Moments later, Gaddafi was dead. Nonetheless, in the face of overwhelming force, loss of control of nearly the entire country, and destruction of nearly his entire military force, he did not surrender nor adhere to demands laid forth by the U.N. Security Council Resolutions.

Coercive Theory Analysis

In the light of historical context and operational actions, the applicability of coercion theory to Operations Unified Protector and Odyssey Dawn becomes possible. The analysis of coercion theory applied to recent coalition operations in Libya encompasses three broad approaches. First, it looks at its distinguishability as a coercive effort from a historical theorist perspective. Next, the analysis applies coercive typologies to operations to determine the nature of the coercive attempt. Finally, it investigates the decision-making process and characteristics necessary for coercion.

Military Operations Recognizable as Coercive Attempt?

Operations Unified Protector and Odyssey Dawn are recognizable as coercive attempts. On the most superficial level, the United Nations, NATO, and the United States seem to have

---

[101]Ibid.

33

used force and the threat of force to bring about a change in Gaddafi's behavior. If coercion through warfare uses an "act of force to compel our enemy to do our will", then Clausewitz would similarly see a coercive attempt. This assumes the desired change of behavior, or "our will", matches the legal basis for action and rhetoric of the coalition as a whole. However, should the desired change of behavior become incongruent with the stated goals of the operations, the foundations of its classification as coercion become shaky or at least murky. For the time being, the distinguishability of the operations as a coercive attempt allows a progression from its classification as a coercive attempt in the broadest sense.

The specific classification of the coercive attempt then hinges on operational characteristics. In other words, should Operations Unified Protector and Odyssey Dawn display characteristics more or less in line with deterrence, compellence, denial, punishment, risk, decapitation or crony attack, then coercive theory can provide an increased understanding of the attempted approach. An identified broad coercive approach enables an analysis of the effectiveness of military operations to affect the decision makers.

The most obvious coercive characterization is Operation Unified Response and Odyssey Dawn as either a compellent or a deterrent military operation. As previously described, compellence seeks to actively alter a target actor's current behavior. Alternatively, deterrence seeks to convince an actor to maintain a status quo. As deterrence would have the unfavorable activity never occur, portions of operations in Libya could be categorized as deterrence. UNSCR 1970 threatened increased sanctions on any individual who threatened or caused increased human rights abuses, specifically attacks and aerial bombardments on civilian populations. Such threats resemble deterrence. Specifically, President Obama's threat on March 17th to dissuade further advance towards Benghazi could be construed as deterrence. Individually viewed, these examples support a deterrent impetus. Yet, the line between deterrence and compellence blurs when military operations commence.

Looking at specific instances of threat or action seeking specific or local outcomes may not fall neatly into a single category. Thus, viewing the operations holistically and in light stated political outcomes helps clarify the character of the coercive attempt. Compellence urges an actor to stop doing an unfavorable activity. UNSCR 1973 demands of the cessation of hostile activity by the government of Libya against its civilian population clearly demonstrate compellence in the broadest sense—stop doing something or face the consequences. The United States' demands for an immediately implemented cease-fire, and cessation of attacks against civilians also qualify as compellence. He furthered a compellence case by specifying exact conditions such as a retreat from Benghazi, Ajdabiya, Misrata, and Zawiya, and the establishment of basic services and humanitarian supplies to all areas. Therefore, in addition to being a positively coercive attempt, the coalition specifically implemented a broad approach of compellence rather than deterrence to stop Gaddafi from attacking and threatening to attack civilians in Libya. The premise of threat and action was cessation of undesirable behavior.

Having determined an apparent compellence approach in Operations Unified Response and Odyssey Dawn, determination of specific strategy can add understanding to the coercive attempt. Specific strategy requires an examination of operations in light of risk, punishment, decapitation, denial and crony attack. Risk, the attempt sway the decision maker by holding the civilian population at risk, can obviously be discounted immediately. Protection of the civilian population, after all, represented the impetus for the operations in the first place. The other possible strategies do not so easily dismiss themselves.

Punishment uses military attacks to deliver a measured amount of pain as a result of the target's undesirable actions. The difficulty remains in the proportionality of destruction and the remaining targets by which the target can still be coerced. Punishment normally bypasses military formations and targets civilian targets or industrial bases. Therefore, in Libya's case, punishment would have been impotent as a counter-value strategy against Gaddafi who did not draw power from his civilian base. Additionally, the revolution, not NATO air forces, threatened his industrial bases. Therefore, either threatening or actually striking civilian or industrial targets would not have worked. Indeed, they were not among the X targets.

Denial strategy, however, did seem to play a significant role in Operations Unified Response and Odyssey Dawn. Denial attempts to destroy, or threaten to destroy, enough military forces as to deny the enemy's strategy. Denial ultimately targets the calculation of the probability of success. Theoretically, when all conceived/conceivable plans become seemingly unattainable, a favorable decision should follow. Gaddafi certainly felt the imposition of coalition power, air power in particular, against his fielded forces. The strikes against X, Y and Z demonstrated the coalition's ability to disrupt command and control, command the air, and protect civilian populations. Having critical capabilities and resources denied, Gaddafi should have rationally come to a favorable decision under the terms and conditions of the UNSCR 1973. The anatomy of decision-making is discussed later. Let it suffice to say that the denial of Gaddafi's capabilities to achieve his strategic military aims had been achieved by coalition strikes.

Decapitation strategy attempts to strike directly at adversary leadership, removing a decision maker from power to allow a favorable decision to be made. In spite of claims to the contrary, the United States has repeatedly tried to conduct decapitation through targeted killing of enemy leadership.[102] Again, here coercion enters murky waters. Perhaps given certain command structures, decapitation of a leader only serves the operational purpose of disrupting command and control and not a leader's decision making in regards to coercion. Would a viable threat against Gaddafi's life result in a desired behavioral change? Apparently not. The X weapons

---

[102]Byman and Waxman, 94. Byman and Waxman discuss decapitation attempts in Libya as part of Operation El Dorado Canyon against Libya. Additionally, the US has targeted residences of Saddam Hussein and Slobodan Milosevic among others. Targeted killing remains a heated discussion, especially as it's used against Al Qaeda leadership. The continued debate demonstrates the America's reticent but pragmatic acceptance of decapitation.

dropped on Gaddafi's personal residence seem to indicate decapitation attempts. Indeed, his ultimate demise resulted from direct targeting of his caravan. But the direct targeting of Gaddafi calls into question the entire coercive intent. If the goal was simply behavioral change, the cessation of hostilities towards civilians, for example, a decapitation strategy of this authoritarian leader demonstrated a belief that no behavioral change was imminent. Decapitation also hints at a fundamentally different goal: regime change as equally as viable, or perhaps equally as desirable, as behavioral change of the regime.[103] The presence of decapitation efforts erodes the assertions of a coercive strategy and favors of a strategy of regime change by brute force.

Having examined Operations Unified Response and Odyssey Dawn in light of coercive strategies, several observations emerge. Namely, punishment and risk, as counter-value strategies, seem to have played very little role as guiding strategies. Rather, elements of denial and decapitation, as counter-force coercive strategies, both apparently played a leading role in the military operations. The presence of denial strategies indicates coercion. Yet aspects of the operations, especially decapitation efforts and lack of decision as a result of denial, raise questions concerning the assumptions that undergird coercion.

Coercion and Decision-Making

Insomuch as Gaddafi behaved tyrannically towards his own, albeit revolting, population, his capability to act as a rational decision maker immediately comes into question. After all, his own destructive behavior spawned the necessity for Operations Odyssey Dawn and Unified Protector. Examining several aspects of decision making and several key points of decision

_____

[103]Ibid., 95. In essence, the authors assert that decapitation can kill but can seldom coerce.

preceding and during the military operations can enhance the understanding of the alleged

coercive effort by coalition forces. Several critical questions must be asked.

First, could Gaddafi be treated as a unitary, rational actor as traditional coercion theory

advocates? Within his own rationale he sought regime and personal survival. He eventually

sought off ramps in the form of ceasefires and political alternatives. Furthermore, given the

authoritarian nature of the Libyan government, a planner might attempt to categorize Gaddafi as a

unitary actor capable of independent decision. Indeed, through the institution of *Jamahiriyya*, or

"state of the people" in 1977, Gaddafi claimed that he truly did not retain power over the people

of Libya. In spite of that, institutions remained tightly under the control of the dictator.[104] In such

a case, a simple application of sticks and carrots against the individual could potentially serve to

elicit a decision. In spite of the power structure, the complexity of the Libyan political

environment provides a more complex understanding of power relationships. Gaddafi's sons

played an important role in the Gaddafi's service and advisement. The importance of his eldest

son, Saif al-Islam, is demonstrated through his orchestration of a June 2011 offer of elections in

which the dictator offered to step down.

Secondly, were the messages and terms clearly communicated and understood? President

Obama insisted that he did not plan to order the use of military force to achieve the political

objective of removing Gaddafi from power. The United Nations, NATO, and USAFRICOM all

emphasized behavior change and either denied or deemphasized regime change. Albeit heads of

state either implicitly or explicitly advocated regime change, the official political documents

---

[104]Mohamed Eljahmi, "Libya and the US: Qadhafi Unrepentant," *Middle East Quarterly* 13, no. 1 (Winter 2006): 12. The author argues that in spite of the establishment of the Basic People's Congresses, People's Committees and because the establishment of the Revolutionary Committees, death squads and Law of Collective Punishment, Qadhafi ruled supreme.

stopped well short of removal of the dictator's removal. Cleary, the international community issued clear communication regarding cessation of hostile actions against the civilian population. Best case, Gaddafi received a mixed message. Worst case, in terms of coercion, Gaddafi received a clear message that was inconsistent with underlying intent.

Finally, were the messages and terms of coercion credible? In other words, was the communicated impetus of military operations authentic? Gaddafi seemed to believe he still possessed an opportunity for a genuine way out. That did not seem to be the case. Gaddafi offered multiple ceasefires before and during military operations to no avail. Gaddafi and his son advocated an opportunity for power transition through popular elections monitored by international observers? The international response, or lack thereof, seemed to indicate that even if he would have modified his behavior in the manner of asking, a cessation of the military operations was off the table.

In terms of decision making, Gaddafi could be considered a single, rational actor in traditional coercion terms. More importantly, that fact seems to be irrelevant to the outcome of Operations Odyssey Dawn and Unified Protector. Even a single, rational actor becomes unpredictable in an unfamiliar situation such as an Arab Spring context amidst mixed messages from international organizations. Coalition messages and terms were not clearly articulated. Apparently, messages and terms were not clearly articulated because the actual strategic aims did not match the stated aims.

Conclusions

This monograph asserts that even though Operations Odyssey Dawn and Unified Protector succeeded in supporting the removal of the Gaddafi regime, ultimately they represent a coercive failure in application as evidenced by a lack of behavioral change by the dictator prior to his death. The United States and NATO continued military attacks while Gaddafi unrelentingly scorned United Nation's resolutions, American policies and NATO's military actions until his death. Logically, if an attacker attempts coercion but the war only ends when the target is decisively defeated, coercion has failed.[105] Coercion, therefore, in the context of Operations Odyssey Dawn and Unified Protector failed.

Pundits hail military actions in Libya as a model for future operations. However, it may better serve as a basis to further an understanding of coercion theory than a template for future action. Coercion theory seeks to affect a desired behavioral outcome through the use of force, threat of force, or concerted use of both. Military operations in Libya had all three components of coercion: force, threat of force and the combinations, thereof. Yet, Gaddafi's stated, desired behavioral outcome never materialized. An answer to the discrepancy may lie in three important realizations from Libyan operations in 2011.

First, in order for coercion to be possible, *the stated desired behavioral change must be intended*. In other words, coercion assumes the intent to coerce. It seems too obvious to state. However, if the communicated and articulated basis for military action is not the actual basis for military action, the target of coercion has no realistic chance of modifying behavior to meet hidden expectations. Academically, regime change is a perfectly legitimate basis for military action. However, regime change, once decided upon especially in an unexpressed manner, leaves no room for coercive behavioral change on the part of the decision maker. In Libya, if absolute regime change provided the true basis for military action, Gaddafi could have never modified his behavior in such a manner so as to satisfy the coercer short of an exile of some sort.

A second realization closely reinforces the first: *coercive demands must contain a plausible way out*. Plausibility applies to both the coerced and the coercer. Certainly, the target

---

[105]Pape, 15.

must be thoroughly considered when crafting and offering off-ramps of behavior. Skillful solutions short of unconditional surrender are the essence of coercion. However, all pertinent coalition members must agree to the acceptability of a solution before its being offered to the target.

In Libya, had Gaddafi withdrew from Benghazi in mid-March, had he stopped using aircraft to attack rebels, had he allowed aid to flow to U.N. specified locations, would coalition members have ceased military operations? In other words, would Gaddafi's compliance with stated demands have resulted in a positive behavioral change? A reflection of ceasefires as a path towards behavioral change becomes instructive. When both the U.N. and the Libyan government alternately offered ceasefires as an off-ramp to the violence that catalyzed the conflict, they were not taken seriously and they subsequently failed. Accusations flew on both sides as to who was to blame for ceasefire failures. The Transitional National Council failed to adhere to ceasefire mandates just as fervently, or more so, than Gaddafi and his forces. The fact remains that the only off ramps towards a peaceful solution in Libya never materialized because no plausible way out was offered. Very likely, certain coalition members and rebels never desired truly desired a peaceful solution. Therefore, no plausible way out ever existed by which Gaddafi could be coerced.

A third realization is that *coalition objectives and agendas must be thoroughly enumerated.* This conclusion resides in both of the previous ones but really takes form in the second. Agendas of the individual partner nations and other major actors must be taken into consideration when considering the ultimate objective of a military operation. This realization also seems obvious. Yet, coalition structures fail to appreciate or at least express the power of individual agendas on the military operation. If agendas of all pertinent actors are not appreciated, reality may not match the stated agendas of even the largest institutions. The United Nations insisted that its interests were purely humanitarian. NATO never publically advocated regime change and quite often insisted to the contrary. However, in the end, if regime change were the

41

guiding principle, it would seem that individual nations and other actors, like the NTC, may have had an inordinate sway on the purpose of military operations, more than the institutions themselves.

The general success of Operations Odyssey Dawn and Unified Protector tempt planners to cling to them as templates for future military operations. The operations were relatively low cost in terms of coalition blood and treasure.[106] It is equally tempting to quickly lump military operations in Libya in 2011 into the growing heap of coercion literature. Especially in light of the 2012 National Military Strategy, planners should be eager to seize lessons of coercion if they were to be found in Libya. Potential coercive examples from this operation promised innovative, low-cost, and small footprint approaches. In this context, denial, punishment, risk, and decapitation remain relevant as far as they are present in some form.

However, Operations Odyssey Dawn and Unified Protector, as a coercive failure, ought not be included in the broad collection of coercive thought. As Pape observed, "Coercion fails when the coercer stops its coercive military actions prior to concessions by the target, when the coercer's attacks continue but do not produce compliance by the target, or when the coercer imposes its demands only after complete defeat of the target."[107] It should be added: coercion fails when coercion was never intended. Military operations did not seek a behavioral change; they sought regime change. They did not offer a true off-ramp for the decision maker. They

---

[106]Jessica Rettig, "End of NATO's Libya Intervention Means Financial Relief for Allies," *U.S. News online*, October 31, 2011, http://www.usnews.com/news/articles/2011/10/31/end-of-natos-libya-intervention-means-financial-relief-for-allies (accessed on September 4, 2012). The eight month military intervention in Libya cost the United States $1.1B with zero American casualties. According to the Congressional Research Service, a single month of military operations in Afghanistan costs the Department of Defense alone more than $6B in that same time period. Amy Belasco, "The Cost of Iraq, Afghanistan, and Other Global War on Terror Operations Since 9/11," *Congressional Research Service online*, March 29, 2011, http://www.fas.org/sgp/crs/natsec/RL33110.pdf (accessed on September 4, 2012).

[107]Pape, 15.

fronted conditional institutional objectives that in reality were absolute and subject to individual and national objectives. As such, Gaddafi had very little opportunity to respond in a meaningful way other than he did: he died.

Perhaps, however, Operations Odyssey Dawn and Unified Protector can still contribute to coercion, in practice, if not in theory. Possibly the most pragmatic contribution to coercion offered by military operations in Libya during 2011 is the reinforcement of emerging international norms of responsible behavior, as Lawrence Freedman asserted. Feasibly, the United States and its allies can bring to bear the credibility wrought by Libya against new would-be Gaddafis who would dare violate an international norm of acceptability. Meanwhile, the United States must recognize that new international norms constantly evolve and change precisely because they are acted upon. Credibility and new behavioral norms, however, do not necessarily translate into contextually successful coercion. In each potential opportunity, coercion is difficult and offers no easy solutions.

Thus, the greatest contribution to coercion theory emerges—a healthy skepticism and caution towards a prescriptive approach towards coercion. An over-simplified, parsimonious theory may be scientifically satisfying but offer very little in terms of real-world application. Accordingly, a danger of coercion theory is an over-reliance on simplicity, reduction and forecasting. For instance, a coercion theory that relies on an interstate construct might be useful in some cases but terribly constricting in most modern operational environments. Conversely, a nuanced, complex theory may be less scientifically satisfying, but provide a stronger starting point for understanding. In other words, terms of coercion theory—such as coercive target, decision-maker, command structure, cultural impact on decision making, etc.—can offer a starting point for asking questions about changing not only behaviors but also conditions in an operational environment. Perhaps instead of addressing the behavioral change of a specific leader, coercion theory can start addressing behavioral change of a state—or system—as a whole.

Clearly, the prospect of addressing systemic behavior as a target of coercion compels military planners to avoid over-simplistic, prescriptive, or reductionist views.

Therefore, appreciation of coercion theory is still critical, especially preceding military operations. However, the expectation of coercion theory providing easy answers starts to recede. Indeed, according to Walter J. Peterson, if policy prescriptions are to be derived from coercion theory, then "the specific conditions under which they may be said to apply need to be sharply specified."[108] Both research and practice reveal that specification is a most difficult task. In other words, the specification of the conditions under which coercion works is doable but difficult.

---

[108]Walter J. Petersen, "Deterrence and Compellence," 287.

BIBLIOGRAPHY

Al Arabiya. "Clash Breaks Out as Libya Braces for Day of Anger." *Al Arabiya online*. February 16, 2011. http://www.alarabiya.net/articles/2011/02/16/137834.html (accessed 27 May 2012).

Al Jazeera. "Gaddafi Defiant as State Teeters." *Al Jazeera online*. February 23, 2011. http://www.aljazeera.com/news/africa/2011/02/20112235434767487.html (accessed on May 28, 2012).

——. "Libyan Opposition Launches Council." *Al Jazeera online*. February 27, 2011. http://www.aljazeera.com/news/africa/2011/02/2011227175955221853.html# (accessed on May 28, 2012).

——. "Nato strike 'kills Gaddafi's youngest son'." *Al Jazeera online*. May 1, 2011. http://www.aljazeera.com/news/africa/2011/04/2011430224755721620.html (accessed on September 6, 2012).

Al-Shalchi, Hadeel and Abbot, Sebastian. "Libya Cease-Fire: South Africa Says Gaddafi Has Accepted African Union 'Road Map'." *Huffington Post online*. http://www.huffingtonpost.com/2011/04/10/libya-cease-fire-road-map_n_847226.html, 20 April 2011 (accessed on September 5, 2012).

Ames, Roger T., ed. and trans. Sun Tzu: *The Art of Warfare*. New York: Ballantine Books, 1993.

Andres, Richard. "When to Target Enemy Heads of State." Paper prepared for the Air Command and Staff College conference on Airpower, Maxwell AFB, AL, Spring 2004.

BBC News. "Libya: US, France and UK attack Gaddafi Forces." *BBC news online.* 20 Mar 2011. http://www.bbc.co.uk/news/world-africa-12796972 (accessed on September 3, 2012).

——. "Muammar Gaddafi: How He Died." *BBC.co.uk*, October 31, 2011. http://www.bbc.co.uk/news/world-africa-15390980 (accessed on March 21, 2012).

——. "NATO Answers Libya Questions."*BBC.co.uk*. Aug 20, 2011. http://www.bbc.co.uk/news/world-africa-14603245 (accessed on March 23, 2012).

Belasco, Amy, "The Cost of Iraq, Afghanistan, and Other Global War on Terror Operations Since 9/11." *Congressional Research Service online*. March 29, 2011. http://www.fas.org/sgp/crs/natsec/RL33110.pdf (accessed on September 4, 2012).

Black, Ian. "Libyan rebels win international recognition as country's leaders." *Guardian online*. July 15, 2011. http://www.guardian.co.uk/world/2011/jul/15/libyan-rebels-international-recognition-leaders (accessed on September 6, 2012).

Blanchard, Christopher, *Libya: Unrest and U.S. Policy*. CRS Report for Congress, Washington D.C.: Congressional Research Service, 29 March 2011.

Bratton, Patrick. "When is Coercion Successful, and Why Can't We Agree On It?" *Naval War College Review* 58, no. 3 (Summer 2005): 99-120.

Burns, John F. "NATO Bombs Tripoli in Heaviest Strike Yet." *New York Times online*. May 23, 2011. http://www.nytimes.com/2011/05/24/world/africa/24libya.html (accessed on August 12, 2012).

Byman, Daniel and Waxman, Matthew. *The Dynamics of Coercion: American Foreign Policy and the Limits of Military Might*. Cambridge, U.K.: Cambridge University Press, 2002.

Christian Science Monitor. "Libya Tribes: Who's Who?" *Christian Science Monitor online*. 24 February, 2011. http://www.csmonitor.com/world/backchannels/2011/0224/Libya-tribes-who-s-who (accessed May 24, 2012).

Clausewitz, Carl von. *On War*. Edited and Translated by Michael Howard and Peter Paret. Princeton, NJ: Princeton University Press, 1976.

CNN Wirestaff. "Gadhafi: We Will Not Surrender, We Will Not Give Up." *CNN online*. June 7, 2011. http://articles.cnn.com/2011-06-07/world/libya.war_1_airstrikes-libyan-officials-nato?_s=PM:WORLD (accessed on August 12, 2012).

Cody, James R. "Coercive Airpower in the Global War on Terror: Testing Validity of Courses of Action." Thesis, School of Advanced Military Studies, 2003.

Daily Mail. "RAF strikes against Gaddafi's forces branded 'a success' as bombed out tanks and cars litter the roads near Benghazi." *DailyMail online*. 20 March 2011. http://www.dailymail.co.uk/news/article-1368028/Libya-RAF-strikes-Gaddafis-forces-branded-success-nearBenghazi.html?openGraphAuthor=%2Fhome%2Fsearch.html%3Fs%3D%26authornamef%3DDaily%2BMail%2BReporters (accessed on 3 September 2012).

Davis, Paul K. *Simple Models to Explore Deterrence and More General Influence in the War with al-Qaeda*. Arlington, VA: RAND Corporation, 2010.

Eljahmi, Mohamed. "Libya and the US: Qadhafi Unrepentant." *Middle East Quarterly* 13, no. 1 (Winter 2006): 11-20.

Fadel, Leila. "Libyan rebels reject African Union cease-fire proposal." *Washington Post online*. April 10, 2011. http://www.washingtonpost.com/world/gaddafi-accepts-road-map-for-peace-proposed-by-african-leaders/2011/04/10/AFbrtuJD_story.html (accessed on September 5, 2012).

Freedman, Lawrence. *Deterrence*. Cambridge, U.K.: Polity Press, 2006.

Gause III, Greg. "Why Middle East Studies Missed the Arab Spring: The Myth of Authoritarian Stability." *Foreign Affairs* 90, no. 4 (July/August 2011): 81-91.

Haun, Phil. "On Death Ground: Why Weak States Resist Great Powers Explaining Coercion Failure in Asymmetric Interstate Conflict." Ph.D. diss., Massachusetts Institute of Technology, 2010.

Interim National Council. "A Vision of a Democratic Libya." *Al Jazeera online*. March 29, 2011. http://www.aljazeera.com/mritems/Documents/2011/3/29/2011329113923943811The%20Interim%20Transitional%20National%20Council%20Statement.pdf (accessed on May 30, 2012).

Moss, Dana and Bruce, Ronald. "Reforming the Rogue: Lessons from the US-Libyan Rapprochement." *The Cutting Edge*. Jan 4, 2010. http://www.thecuttingedgenews.com/index.php?article=11878&pageid=13&pagename=Analysis (accessed on June 1, 2012).

Mueller, Karl. "The Essence of Coercive Air Power: A Primer for Military Strategists," *Air Power Journal* 2, no. 1 (Spring 2007): 159-174.

NATO. *Fact Sheet: Operation UNIFIED PROTECTOR Protection of Civilians and Civilian-Populated Areas & Enforcement of the No-Fly Zone*. http://www.nato.int/cps/en/natolive/71679.htm. (accessed on 28 May 2011).

Pape, Utz. "Interventions Against a Dictator." *Journal of international Affairs* 65 (Fall/Winter 2011): 221-223.

Pape, Robert A. *Bombing to Win: Air Power and Coercion in War*. Ithica, N.Y.: Cornell University Press, 1996.

Petersen, Walter J. "Deterrence and Compellence: A Critical Assessment of Conventional Wisdom." *International Studies Quarterly* 30, no.3. September 1986. http://www.jstor.org/stable/2600418 (accessed 1 May, 2012).

Raghaven, Sudarson and Fadel, Leila. "Military Helicopters Reportedly Fire on Protesters in Libya." *Washington Post online*. February 21, 2011. http://www.washingtonpost.com/wp dyn/content/article/2011/02/20/AR2011022004185.html (accessed on May 27, 2012).

Rettig, Jessica. "End of NATO's Libya Intervention Means Financial Relief for Allies." *U.S. News online*. October 31, 2011. http://www.usnews.com/news/articles/2011/10/31/end-of-natos-libya-intervention-means-financial-relief-for-allies (accessed on September 4, 2012).

Rueters. "NATO forces destroy 25 Libyan tanks." *DefenceWeb online*. April 11, 2011. http://www.defenceweb.co.za/index.php?option=com_content&view=article&id=14711: nato-forces-destroy-25-libyan-tanks&catid=50:Land&Itemid=105 (accessed on September 5, 2012).

Schelling, Thomas C. *Arms and Influence*. New Haven, CT: Yale University Press, 1966.

Tolbert, Julian. "Crony Attack: Strategic Attack's Silver Bullet?" Thesis, School of Advanced Military Studies, 2003.

Thucydides. *History of the Peloponnesian War*. New York: Penguin, 1954.

United States Africa Command. "AFRICOM Commander on Commencement of Military Strikes in Libya." *USAFRICOM Public Affairs Release*. 19 March 2011. http://www.africom.mil/getArticle.asp?art= 6222&lang=0 (accessed on 28 May, 2011).

—. "Overview of 1st Day of U.S. Operations to Enforce U.N. Resolution 1973 Over Libya." *USAFRICOM Public Affairs Release*. 20 March 2011. http://www.africom.mil/ getarticle.asp?art=6237& (accessed on 28 May, 2011).

United States Department of Defense. "DOD News Briefing with Vice Adm. Gortney from the Pentagon on Libya Operation Odyssey Dawn." Office of the Secretary of Defense (Public Affairs). 19 March 2011. http://www.defense.gov/transcripts/transcript.aspx?transcriptid=4786 (accessed on 4 September 2012).

—. *Joint Publication 1-02, Dictionary of Military and Associated Terms*. Washington D.C.: Government Printing Office: 8 November 2010 (Amended through 15 July 2012).

—. *Sustaining U.S. Global Leadership: Priorities for 21st Century Defense*. Washington, DC: Government Printing Office: January 2012.

United States Mission to the United Nations, *Fact Sheet: New UN Security Council Resolution on Libya*, http://usun.state.gov/briefing/statements/2011/158614.htm, (accessed on 28 May, 2012).

—. *Fact Sheet: UN Security Council Resolution 1970, Libya Sanctions*. http://usun.state.gov/ briefing/statements/2011/157194.htm (accessed on 28 May, 2012).

USA Today. "Anti-government Protesters Killed in Libyan Clash." *USA Today online*. February 17, 2011. http://www.usatoday.com/news/world/2011-02-17-libya-protests_N.htm (accessed on May 27, 2012).

Vira, Varun and Cordesman, Anthony H. "The Libyan Uprising." *Center for Strategic and International Studies*. June 2011. http://csis.org/publication/libyan-uprising-uncertain-trajectory (accessed on 6 September 2012).